REVEALING TO HEALING

A Poetic Journey from Wounds to Wisdom

Judith E Maynard

ISBN 978-0-9975042-9-3
Library of Congress Control Number 2022903524

Printed and bound in the United States of America
First Printing March 2022

Editing, book cover design, and interior formatting by:
Dean Diaries Publishing

To order additional copies of this book, contact the author:
Judith Maynard
queenjuju2018@gmail.com

Table of Contents

Dedication

Thank God for this opportunity, and the talents he created in me.

To my mom (Tillie Austin) who made me steadfast and unmoveable, my big brother Gary Maynard for cheering for me, my sister Patricia Sherrod, my niece Arnisha Lark, who kept me focused and inspired through many of my poems. My auntie Elaine Rankin, cousin Sophia Spraggins for listening to me and reading my literary content, my dear friend Lameka Blackmon, Samore Haynes Sherrod, Terri Alford, Theresa M Paul, and my DPD family from Detroit. Also a special shout out to the Freedom Equity Group for giving me the courage to be authentically myself.

ABUSE CALLED DISCIPLINE

Cracked across the back so hard, you must comply.

No questions asked, many tears to cry.

Keep those negros in line, compliance is a must.

Ruled by fear from dawn to dusk.

Once the mind is overpowered it's easy to rule, no talking back, you must be a fool.

Generationally cursed humans beaten into submission, stolen from their homeland for profit, without permission.

Treated like animals, subjected to humiliation, just do like you're told.

Bought and paid for from birth until you are old.

Life as a slave never set right the African in bondage, a new language to learn, no culture, new religion, remain held hostage.

Terrorism is quite real in America, yet only for blacks.

The excessive use of force called discipline justified these attacks.

Considered property not worth more than a horse, a horrific new life had taken its course.

Beginning in 1619 near Jamestown Virginia, free labor began, an entire country stolen and rebuilt forced on the African.

Accepting the despicable exploitation, unlivable conditions, a mindset was now changed into normal traditions.

Shackled, whippings became a way of life, inherently sufficient suffering strife.

As the plantations grew larger, the need for more slaves was relevant.

The more the slaves reproduced, the more workers were evident.

Continuing this brutality for over 300 years, degraded, bodies mutilated, obedience in place by their fears.

Though many attempted to escape to no avail captured, treated even worse.

Still a hunger for freedom overwhelmed for the thirst.

Held captive originating from physical abuse, then redirected mentally, verbally misuse.

Forbidden to read, write or move without restrictions, told they were inferior unable to learn an obvious contradiction.

Throughout history lies have been told, the value of the black family is worth more than gold.

Stigma and shame have destroyed an entire nation.

Ridiculed, murdered without hesitation.

Passing down horrendous tools to stagnate control, by inhumane assertion.

Oppressing the mind to believing this display was correcting the person.

Many black families believe by whipping you convey dominance enforcing your authority.

This demeaning behavior only hardens the soul, damages the majority.

Enslavement in itself causes a breakdown in the spirit, the mental attacks like name-calling, garnished with inferior complexes in it.

Discipline in its reality is correction by love, not by diminishing your character, like being drug through the mud.

The practice of mishandling a foundation stemming from greed, the brokenness of a nation.

Still being perpetuated in many homes and the police station.

Overcoming by truth is the way to the healing, retribution inequality a standard no more concealing.

Giving all humans a fair shake, no more of these dirty dealings.

The damage is done, you can't take back what's done in our past, yet a second chance can be given in love guaranteed it will last.

Stop the abuse justifying by the evil within, hurting people in this manner is not discipline.

ANCESTORS

Our culture, our heritage, the way we use to live, what
happened to helping each other, the way we use to give.

Generations together, residents of the same house,
combining our goods, no one goes without.

Where are the families with dad leading, mothers caring for
children, and succeeding?

Being close to my cousins, no jealousy, no competing.

The consciousness of our spirits is no longer as strong, too
afraid to admit mistakes continuing to be wrong.

Pride has corrupted our thinking; we're easily persuaded
without even blinking.

The residue of our messiness is lingering and stinking.

Protecting women no longer a priority, men have softened
more often a large majority.

Who can our children expect to guide their feet, it's hard to
look up when they lay down dying in the street?

They have given up and accepted defeat.

It's everywhere no more discrete.

We don't give up our chairs to give the elderly a seat.

Disrespecting the sacrifice our ancestors made is evident, pathways destroyed from self-serving attitudes are relevant.

We should never forget but have a memory like an elephant.

Their struggles should bring light to our haste, yet we continue in behaviors distressed while time we did waste.

Materialistic, so consumed with things, not concerned with what a negative mindset brings.

We've come away from disciplining ourselves, blaming our conduct on everybody else.

Maturity, accountability, humility have all gone to hell.

The endurance of our ancestors was relentless, their countenance did not fail.

We must bring back to life a vision, take inventory of ourselves, make the decision.

Greatness was given, we must change our ways of living.

The prayers of many righteous were manifestors, Lord gives us a resilient spirit with the strength of our ancestors.

ANGER

Intensely ravenous are the flames, provoked energy unprofitable as it remains.

Creating hostile inflections, only hatred explains.

Holding hostages never wanting to be contained.

Explosive outburst ridiculing all who is named.

Touching the fire intrigued by its aim.

A decision was made in haste I exclaimed.

Repeatedly inviting the attraction, unfulfilling with no satisfaction, the perspective in my mind a misguided contraption.

Lashing out while unwilling, spewing words in anger like I'm killing, the enemies residing in me, an unrighteous feeling.

Bad behavior is trending for lack of dealing, my issues of life causing a persona unappealing.

Stuck in a position that's familiar yet appearing safe.

Unable to move forward fearing the reflection of my own face.

Giving into emotions controlled by my anger, letting me know my life is in danger.

All too often I'm found wearing a mask, nevermind what I'm actually feeling, don't bother to ask.

I've bottled up tightly inside resembling, forever remembering these chains from my past.

It is what it is, I'm used to the pain, I say one thing then back to old behavior again.

A toxic cycle has me trapped in my own head, there have been times when I wished I was dead, thank God he had greater plans for my life instead.

There's a need for healing, necessary as resting in my bed.

Screaming frantically, wondering what happened to me, my personality.

Desperately craving just to be loved, the kind you can feel warm from a hug.

Mad as hell always fighting, forbidden turf I'm always hiding.

For years I've seen myself as the stranger, conflicted in bondage by my ferocious anger.

ARE YOU REALLY READY?

What's the hurry when it's not a designation, going fast without navigation, rushing towards harsh abbreviations, troubling to the soul through frustrations.

Being in the way causing best efforts to fail, objectifying through clouded perspectives not able to set sail.

Being your own worst enemy completely ready to bail.

The yearning that has you burning, constantly chasing your tail.

Stepping out of one mindset into another changes the disparity applied yet moving no further.

The plan for your life is out of your hands, trusting in the one not time is what life demands.

Are you really ready or just running according to a schedule echoing commands?

Desire is necessary essentially though unknown to where it lands.

Timing along with maturity is not forsaken but security.

Managing to have acceptance and patience reaching goals assuredly.

Undetected reasoning factors in the trust, doubt mixed with stubbornness blocks blessings guaranteed to us.

Waiting for the opportunity being unmovable is a must.

Though your intentions are strong, what you think you possess won't reside with you long.

Actually, receiving it too early when you're not ready is wrong.

Too many occasions with you singing the same song.

Finally understanding you put yourself in a place you didn't belong.

Nurturing the spirit is freedom for pathways, giving into your flesh corrupts our best days.

Releasing bad vibes like burning cigarettes in ashtrays.

Take the time that's needed, use what's inside of you, and be completed.

There's food for thought now eat it.

Struggling will be cut in half when you stop dwelling on scenarios from your past.

Occasions may come often and steady, yet ask yourself before you react, are you really ready?

BE THE VIBE YOU DESIRE

Scented candles, aromas wafting sending memories of the warmth you bring.

Sunset's captivating, your touch like the first day of spring.

Communicating rhythmic messages felt by the strength of your tone.

Confident you'll always be in my spirit never left alone.

Listening when I need your ear, gently your hand wipe's my tear.

Sympathetic and empathetic in tune to what I need, whether it be my body, my soul, or mind, you concede.

Thoughtfully anticipating, seeming as though you can read my mind.

Never do you leave me waiting, you're always on time.

Even through rough patches, we laugh it off by forgiving.

Looking forward to seeing your face every day in my living.

Considerate attitude that never lies about what your feeling, you don't raise your voice or act unyielding.

Courageous with loyalty forever having my back.

Your energy is infectious, you bring balance, keeps me on track.

Praying together consistently, worship is a priority, giving praise to the highest authority.

The essence of your nature is kind and loving, spirits linked and aligned while we're hugging.

Ambitious, ready to face the trials that do come to distract.

Remaining focused, protecting me from any attack.

Being in love is easy with you, uncompromising satisfying, and true, it's us against the world, overcoming obstacles as we subdue.

Passionate in the attraction feeling the heat from your fire.

Sensually, you accessorize my inner attire.

Hypnotically entranced, nothing about you can bore me, having all of my attention, like an eagle I'm soaring.

You touch my soul with so much charisma, charming and clever.

Dear God let this last forever.

You make me better wanting more for myself, positioning me to see how real love is felt.

I'm grateful to you for all I acquire, being taught by you to be the vibe you desire.

BEYOND THE SURFACE

Troubled little girl, lost in a world, attempting to find her way.

Looking into many faces as she travels day today.

Afraid of not being good enough, appearing strong, rugged, and rough, although her heart is damaged, acting to seem tough.

Her fragile stature mirrored with bad behavior.

Struggling in all of her relationships, searching for a savior.

Needing and wanting, having a unique flavor.

Different without an occasion unable to fit in.

Bending over backward trying to win a friend.

What you see is far from me, I'll pretend, to be what you want me to be.

I never felt that I was worth much, my problems began when feeling worthless.

Wore many masks exposing nothing beyond the surface.

Abandonment issues plagued me, low self-esteem continually displayed by me.

Unable to trust, many decisions based on lust, equating sex with love was a must.

Inappropriately navigating through distraught emotions, contemplating my next move through a thought or notions, the span of my pain deeper than all the oceans.

Women like me are used to the ways life hurts us, bottling up those feelings of hopelessness converts us.

Turning us into lost souls afraid of living beyond the surface.

Stemming back to childhood trauma, remembering being told I was overly affectionate from my mama.

Rooted in fear, elevated by my adverse drama.

Emersed deeper into a protective cover, bringing more light as I exchanged another lover.

The closer you try to get to me the more I'd run further, simply yearning for validation not received from my mother.

Filling up my empty room, perpetuating more sadness leading to my doom.

Exhausted by what's described as fleeting gloom.

A lifetime of hurt, angry with myself.

Blaming everything outside of me or someone else.

Fingers pointing back at me brought my spirit out of denial, learning patience has elevated pain causing a change in my style.

Not unwilling to be by myself for a while.

Noticing a difference, no longer chained to a fortress, finding me as I'm revealing more beyond the surface.

BLACK AMERICAN BLUES...

America, America the land of the free, your prices are high, taking lives for centuries.

No black signatures on the Declaration of Independence, can't celebrate on the Fourth of July because of what my ancestors witnessed.

Sick and tired of being abused and neglected, smiling faces with hate in their hearts traditionally projected, yet have the nerve to call us animalistic, blacks always subjected.

Cruelty a usual behavior from the man is expected.

From the time they landed here no love detected.

A veteran gets treated the worse, some gave their lives on this segregated turf.

Can't go to the hospital for anything major without emptying your purse.

Through the eyes that I see it seems like being black is a curse, you stand up to racist police, might end up in a hearse.

We've been lied to since the beginning, even when some of my ancestors were here first.

I served my country proudly, yet we are hated all over this Earth.

I can't understand a love for a flag, in a country that throws away its own like an old rag.

Killing a black person is like playing tag.

Got more love for animals is such a drag, you act like you don't know why we're mad.

Supporting traditions leaving out the entire story, claiming victories, without us they'd have no glory.

Enough is enough my soul is in pain, for repeated atrocities happening again.

Venting your frustrations in America being black you might die, it's the way it is, sometimes we cry.

Our loved ones stood tall fighting wars, being used has been our duty like chores.

Why can't I celebrate my culture like you do yours?

Keeping secrets of criminal behavior behind closed doors.

Only if your white are you free for that right, blacks must go through way more.

It's not an excuse but by design, we were meant to remain poor.

Wealth gaps are staggering, only 1% of the people are rich, things would be different if that wealth in the black community would shift.

We didn't pick this battle nor are we accepting crumbs that don't uplift.

Frankly we are tired of this.

You can't understand unless you've walked in my shoes, nor are you able to explain in good conscience black American blues.

BLACK QUEEN

I see you for your dazzle, the shine in your smile, reeking of courageous stamina, a relentless style.

Unappreciated, subjected to ridicule in spite of tenacity.

Been a part of a struggle that's been destined for a catastrophe.

Holding together the world on your shoulders from the beginning of time.

Considered only a bedwarmer or entertainment yet unkept and conveniently left behind.

Still, you stand like a banner of honor, nothing on this planet is more beautiful or stronger.

BLACK QUEEN you've been sent down from the Heavens to aide and complete.

Though your purpose is rendered thoughtlessly, verbally abused, attacked in your sleep.

You rise above, beyond the transparent images falsely given, healing those you love intentionally, a nurturing decision.

Framed in definition exuding boldness without regret, dignified with amazing gentleness impossible to forget.

BLACK QUEEN we see you walking with your head held high, infinitely built for greatness a design unbreakable the reason why.

Amazingly engaging your fortitude is unable to deny.

You were necessarily needed fulfilling a position only you can handle, the light through a window flickering igniting sensuously illuminating like a candle.

Procreation was and is impossible without you there would be no life on earth, replenishing constantly misrepresented scornfully at birth.

BLACK QUEEN majestic exquisitely formed a radiance seen when you enter a room.

Flawlessly you were made no reason to assume.

Made from love genuinely unique embodied with strength that will remain, subdued yet never able to contain, driving the oppressed forces insane.

Your black man is meant to thrive and provide for you, protect, walk hand in hand, standing side by side with you.

BLACK QUEEN your reputation hasn't been adequately adored, selfishly you've been misused knocked to the floor.

Sympathized with no recognition, evasively ignored.

There will come a time when your glorious presence may be seen, nothing can change the fact of the matter, you are a BLACK QUEEN.

BROTHER I SEE YOU

Your face riddled with stress, contorted from frustration.

Attempting to hide your pain.

Masking years of carrying overwhelming struggles carried inside of you, yet you remain.

Publicly forced into submission, characterized like an animal, misused, and abused.

Still displaying your strength, working harder than all others, your imagery has the oppressor amused, although confused.

Intimidating at first sight, without speaking a word, objectified before being heard.

The fear of you is obviously the penetrating factor unrealistic and absurd.

BROTHER I SEE YOU

Desiring to live in peace even when constantly defeated, crimes thrust upon you, over and over, again repeated.

Managing to hold your head high through experiencing emasculating obstacles, you are a man.

Regardless of what is said about you, doing the best that you can.

Navigating through situations purposely to dismantle, opposition on every side, still you continue moving forward, unspeakable endurance has to be applied.

Courageously ambitious remaining positive, walls knocked down though access is denied.

BROTHER I SEE YOU

It seems as though being you automatically there is a fight, no matter how much good you impose, your redirected, not enough never right.

Resilience defines the nature of your brilliant stature, unmitigated lies are told, false propaganda ridiculously manufactured.

Systems put in place holding you to a different standard regulating by design, how you made it through that last episode completely blows their mind.

Adversaries try to break you, blame you unjustly, rename you when they didn't make you.

Successfully you remain on your feet, the odds were meant to take you.

BROTHER I SEE YOU

Representing, influencing a legacy formed before leaving the womb, the plan to destroy your vision a mindset employed to consume.

Continually bombarded, God's blessings overpower and make room.

You're a threat that can't be broken, undeniably words left unspoken, referred to as a token.

These tests and trials are only for a season, created in greatness, your value is priceless perpetuating the reason.

Jealousy, envious of the fact, unable to perform like you do, be encouraged, continue unapologetically, BROTHER I SEE YOU.

CANCER SELLS

Unexplainable, terrifying, rendering hopelessness without enough of an answer.

Medical treatment charging ridiculously, still the question, "How do you cure cancer?"

Stealing our loved ones, surviving unimaginable, both sides feeling anxiety and pain.

Treatments hurting more than the disease, unable to eat, doctors prescribing medicine, unable to explain.

Where does it really come from, what's the root of its power.

Why do some last for years, months, and others only survive for hours?

Money is spent, millions of dollars being used for research, pastors laying hands on desperate souls yearning, hoping to be healed at the church.

Some believe it's in what we eat, they say the cure can be found in our diet.

Yet when pharmaceutical companies hear of natural methods healing, their first response is don't try it.

Claiming medicine is the only cure, still so many are dying.

I'm beginning to think it's all about money and somebody is lying.

This debilitating illness, you watch your loved ones slowly struggling, attempting to be strong.

Facing the reality that the life you have may not last long.

Though making the best of a difficult obstacle there are those who do pull through.

Then from out of nowhere, it's back again, frustrated without answers, asking God, "Why you?"

Questionably I ask, "If so many have this diagnosis, why on earth are the treatments so extreme yet costly?"

To have health insurance seems hypocrisy, I'm confused you've lost me.

Radiation burns you on the inside, chemo destroys good and bad cells.

Losing your hair, fingernails and non-essentials displaying, deterioration expels.

As time moves on in this life, more seem to become stricken.

Still, no answers in sight, the cure, apparently somewhere far from finding, obviously distant.

I keep praying, my loved one is in a fight, enduring this suffering, not much sleep at night.

Pretending while in denial the facts that won't erase.

So many people are losing to a horrendous illness, running a financial burden, unyielding race.

Universal health care is a topic politicians evade without regret.

Shamefully with high salaries ineffective, the people they neglect.

Until we find a solution it appears cancer treatment will be big business, only money compels.

The research continues, motivating factor, cancer sells.

CONFIDENCE THROUGH BELIEVING

As I clean my minds windows, still looking to see what's next.

Fearing nothing while moving forward, opinions aren't considered to what they may suggest.

Deep inside searching for the strength, unmovable and unkempt.

Believing in the process, with patience maintaining, refusing to get upset.

Trusting for what I'm seeking, in due season I'm still moving closer to what I'll get.

Haven't seen my best days yet, investing having no regret, revelation revealing how much I've been blessed.

As I search through murky residue left from life's mess, celebrating all that I learn while building muscle passing each test.

Smiling while sometimes crying, staying focused on being happy more, not less.

Relying completely on the source which continuously feeds me, believing in myself, by his grace it freed me.

At times I suffer yet my ability is sustained never fleeting, thank God for the stripes on his back, the spiritual meals I'm eating.

Resting better now, let me tell you how, giving no energy to evil distractions repetitiously repeating.

Having breath in my body my momentum proceeding.

Purposed filled on life's journey, lacking nothing sealed because of the bleeding.

Scars reminding and motivating the move towards succeeding.

There's more to me than what you're seeing, greatness in my soul beautifully being.

Loving myself first gave me the confidence through believing.

CRY BABY

Weeping willows softly blowing, rain is falling though not from the skies.

Rays of sun piercing through clouds while tears drop from my eyes.

Footprints leaving tracks molded in the sand, oceans overflowing with wet hands, sun-drenched days far off in distant lands.

My mind overwhelmed by memories saddened, unreasonable thinking does push past what's actually happened.

Nothing that can be put into mere words, yet thoughts of taking flight, soaring higher than all the birds.

Provoking the same questioning, inside my soul is reckoning, better days will come to me maybe, for now, I am a cry baby.

Torn between events taking my thoughts to super lows, manifesting emotional behaviors without rest that flows.

Storms twisting deranged motions, unexplained notions, the stronger wind blows.

Anticipating the length of this invisible disaster, heart pounding like drumbeats striking much faster.

Contemplating a way out to a plan I must master.

Until I find strength I've been drowning here lately, insignificantly as it is, I'm still a cry baby.

Pouring out my soul like spilled milk on the floor.

Walking in darkness hitting walls searching for the door, one that leads to my sorrow no more.

Impatiently awaiting on shorelines dreading the current river brings an uncertain undertow, illusions vastly mistaken as a rescue forbidding me to go.

Beyond the equinox, this crisis type of enemy, resolving what's gotten into me.

The slaying of this dragon unlocks the part in my heart preparing for a fresh start.

Leaving behind unsavory practices that made me, continuously uncontrollably act like a cry baby.

Growing with discernment adding value to each lesson, essentially being honest leaving nothing for guessing.

Peeling off the layers in my purest confession.

A butterfly freed from the cocoon arrayed by beauty displayed in its new dressing.

Surpassing contorted reflections purposed only to slay me, entranced by improved images comforting and quieting the cry baby.

EMOTIONALLY ON PURPOSE

Multiple emotions, swimming in your mind like raging oceans, through insecurities wanting to be validated, tired of behavior being atrocious.

Confusion reeks whenever your inside voice speaks.

Unable to shake the unmerited fear, unexplainable vibes in your ear, making it difficult to hear.

You find yourself grasping, where hope should appear.

The vision is relative, yet oh so clear.

One minute you're crying, your insides feel like you're dying.

Trapped in a mirrored image falsely.

Reality in reverse almost lost me.

Had to readjust the mindset, consequences too costly.

Making decisions when emotionally unstable is like stacking glasses on a 3 legged table.

Your truth being misguided, turning reality into a fable.

What you should be doing you're not able.

The search continues, looking for your perfected venues, hearts being an open book, like restaurants with open menus.

Still not satisfied, grossly intense.

The moral of the story not yet making sense.

Seeing yourself through clouded windows, tossed around however the wind blows.

Your caught off guard occasionally, thoughts from the past from what used to be.

Decide to look forward to keep from going absolutely crazy.

Story's do have happy endings, depicted in positive vibes transcending.

Knowing you're not breaking, only bending.

Learning from situation to situation, lessons learned by pain in minor abbreviations, new experiences bringing celebrations.

Expectations remain through self-preservations.

Better conclusions digging further than the surface, ultimately, accepting you're emotionally on purpose.

ENERGY VAMPIRE...

You come for free you're not for hire, yo ass driven by Satan, you call him Sire.

Lurking about yearning to encamp itself onto a victim, a soul unaware of the intent to get them.

Understand it's in his plan if you can live once they suck you.

Be prepared for it's in their evil nature to savagely abduct you.

Darkness leading them by night, traces of enticing tactics to insight, fulfilling a never-ending bottomless appetite.

These demonic vessels compelled to increase their forces, armies bloodthirsty pimps, using images as resources.

Blatantly lying portraying an illusion resembling truth, plotting wicked plans beguiling an entire generation beginning as a youth.

Promising while pretending, falsely believing you're not the borrower when lending.

Compromising decisions made in haste instead of defending, manipulating circumstances that come contending.

Recognize their style hidden by that phony smile, wanting you to be totally depending.

Camouflaged in a falsified yet pleasing to the eye, a doomed ending.

Causing your life to ride faster than a rollercoaster, experiencing catastrophic incidents that you're not supposed to.

Only to sustain must they replenish from a living being.

Any lengths exposes the objective no matter how obscene.

Fortified by your energy by any means.

Observe your surroundings the people you engage daily, pay attention to their ways, contrary ordinarily.

Systematic opportunists creating an unrealistic façade.

Alluring captivated you give them the nod, stuck in this position got you calling for God.

Tricked again by a repeated game, the rules never different, you just reacted the same.

Don't make it easy for the attack, be strong as you aspire, behind every corner is waiting an, energy vampire.

Weak links in search of tricks and treats, devouring your lack of stamina, intentionally it defeats.

Smelling of fear resonating its odor, desirable like sweets.

Fooling you regularly a tendency as it completes.

Sunrise vastly coming assuredly its known, the light of its rays too hot when shown.

Missions are strategized in lovely attire, beware of its desire, the energy vampire.

EXPOSED BY THE REFLECTION

Why are we more angry when black people are killed by police, yet we sit back in silence, doing nothing to stop the violence, consistently without cease.

Funeral homes filled to capacity with casualties, a daily increase.

Yet there is zero-tolerance for law enforcement, them killing us seems more important.

Whose redirecting our young black people, who endorse them, crimes set up by design forcing them to engage in unethical behavior, a reckless course for them.

Standing in long lines for a pair of shoes, no resources available by teaching in love without judgment is being used.

Unconsciously without respect for our sister and brother, can't be found in others.

It begins with educating the babies, honoring our fathers and mothers.

Treating our Kings and Queens lovingly should be as natural as breathing, how long shall we keep going on continuously mistreating.

When the neighbor was removed leaving the blight of the hood, now normalized in our vision no remorse a course set for no good.

Black people even those like family, competing mistreating intentionally mishandling.

Yet we stand in the masses shouting black lives matter, I'm confused and not understanding.

Generational curses don't come without a cause, tell these young black men, pull up your pants, no one wants to see your draws.

Communities banning together supporting each other will bring on applause.

Being a living example displaying positivity, stop pointing fingers uplift the cause.

Be the reason we rewrite some laws.

Actively participating in the political process, refusing to ignore the ongoing nonsense.

It's been long overdue yet needs to be said, if we continue in these unprofitable practices, we continue to be misled.

Some is not enough, all should take a seat at the table, lending a hands to those in circumstances who aren't able.

Obviously, there is systemic racism, we see it live and on TV, thank God for the advancement in modern technology.

For without it, our struggle remains with voices not heard, intentionally, completely void.

There would not have been a conviction of the officer who killed George Floyd.

Many now being exposed, misconduct revealed, displaying the numerous lives being destroyed.

As a people with many talents, intelligent, brilliantly gifted.

The time is now for us to keep us uplifted.

Empowering to making ways extending our helpful hands.

Devising a new normal for all people, treated with dignity, rewriting old plans.

Honesty is essential mirrored in our inspection.

Seeing the truth in ourselves, exposed by the reflection.

FREE YOUR MIND

Happiness never began in a place, actually it appeared in the space.

The soul of you, inside of perspective, what you believe or not, your choice, selective.

Past experiences can shape your decisions, based on how you've felt can cause collision.

Emotions don't determine what abides for your purpose, characteristics, statistics only persuade on the surface.

Digging deep, not letting go can stagnate the process to move.

How you respond is free will, you get to choose.

Operating in feelings alone is a journey hard-fought.

The price sometimes inferior, contagious, a negative thought.

We buy our time in rhythmic motions in dealing with people we meet, how we love each other, how we handle defeat.

Perception determines which way we follow, the light or the darkness, a concept we inherently allow.

Perseverance in life motivates, drives us, confronting issues we test, risky, or leaving us average, compared to the rest.

Personally esteemed or objectively we give in the brain.

It operates in patterns, the way it's trained.

Positive conditions may soften some of the traitorous positions, we contend.

Overprotecting the heart, fear, the reason we sometimes pretend.

Delusional pictures barricade the perimeter, replaying the time.

Misplaced emotional upheaval finding ways to redirect freedom in the mind.

Freedom is an objective way of thinking, relatively influenced in part, occasionally we accept concepts as they are, advocated from the heart.

Senseless battles we fight, hoping to win just by our might.

Yet, blindly stepping forward we exhaust all efforts attempting to extend.

True blissful happiness, residing patiently within.

Frequently wasting time on situations familiar, knowing our oppositions, behaving the same overtly, continuing in similar repetitions.

Hopefully, through honesty, self-love, a point in which we are esteemed.

Grasping further than we have before, fulfilling our predestined dreams.

Exposing ourselves vulnerably to that hidden hollowed place, remarkably traced back generationally to our ancestor's face.

I can see it, no rationalization or excuses, only to believe, I can be it.

Removing doubt, the blocking forces preventing me, superficial, so unkind.

Finally found the ability when God said, " Free Your Mind."

There is no more room for confusion when you're not eluded by the illusions.

You set the pace for positive vibes, it's how hard you try, which determines the strive.

Illuminating light will lead you, guiding you with insight.

Circumstances teaches lessons as long as you learn.

Activation, when the time is right, it's now your turn.

Being prepared, stay in your lane, experience will remind.

Everything is possible when you free your mind.

A mustard seed of faith is all that it takes, the proclamation is done, you make no more mistakes.

Confidence, authority, in boldness you declare your demands.

All that you need is inside of you, made by God's hands.

Wisdom is profitable with knowledge you'll succeed, doubting nothing, you've got all that you need.

Living generously, loving intensely, sowing seeds carefully and kind.

Effortlessly new beginnings, when you free your mind.

GONE TO SOON

Never are we ready to let go of the best part, afraid of being alone no love, a broken heart.

What do we do when time moves too quickly, taking you away, how do we accept that you're gone, facing another day?

Memories having me staring off into space, imaginary visions of your face, nothing can replace.

I remember thinking you needed me, fact is I need you to breathe, I wish you could hear me.

Tear-stained pillow with traces of my sadness, trying to make sense of this is madness.

Loving your presence was a blessing that kept me guessing.

You're gone now I'm reassessing, I should have held you closer, now that I'm confessing...gone way too soon...I don't wanna go outside, the sun reminds me of you.

Missing you so bad I'm not sure of what to do.

You're always on my mind especially at night, lately trying to go to sleep is a battle I can't fight.

They say in time healing makes it easier the pain ceases, until that happens I have all these broken pieces.

Mad at the world depression runs deep.

Memories of your face is all that I keep.

Hidden in my heart sweetly protected in a special place, not even time will be able to erase...gone too soon...God will keep me strong in him I put my trust, I feel as though I have nothing left, so I must.

Prepare for a new life until I see you again, remaining a priority my beloved friend.

I won't ever take for granted what I've been given.

Showing unconditional love as long as I'm living.

Each person that takes up space is valued in my life.

They won't be surprised at me saying I love you once or twice.

They will know how important they are without question.

Be good to those who you love is a valued suggestion...gone too soon...so give me my flowers, tell me that you love me hours after hours.

Let it rain like springtime showers.

I will love hard as the sun rules the day and the night has the moon.

Having no regrets or sorries to say, not wanting to get in the way, I'll miss you every day...Gone too soon.

HELD ON WHEN LOVE WAS GONE

The sun rose and set on your fragrance a game pretending, love flowed freely in the beginning, suggesting never-ending.

Fluttering butterflies inside my heart beating, excited from the first-time meeting.

A glance sending chills as you gaze intensely, anxiously awaiting for you to kiss me.

Feeling every part of you, seeing your heart as a work of art needing you.

Wanting you for myself alone, having a kindred spirit with passion unknown.

Your energy changed and love faded, blamed myself when love seemed jaded.

I thought this was forever, thought we should have made it.

Fantasies left broken pieces to a spirit now gated.

Never saw this coming so blissfully blind, just took for granted that you'd always be mine.

But like the seasons changed, your passion for me now estranged.

Tried forcing what should be automatic, destroyed me for a moment, so traumatic.

Losing your love was like kicking a drug habit.

Still determined that time would erase, clinging to a fantasy I willingly embraced, unconsciously the more I'd chase, a dream hidden in a forbidden place.

Letting go seemed impossible to do, every song and most of my memories bring thoughts of you.

Countless years passing before me, obsessing still pressing you sometimes ignored me.

Not even mishandling me would let me give up, overwhelmed with wanting you missing your touch.

Embarrassed from my own behavior lost in disgust, leaving this broken cycle eventually a must.

Stayed lonely behind this episode, enough is enough not able to trust.

Thinking of the time I spent, wondering where my soul went.

From which level of hell were you sent.

Obviously, a lesson to be learned is what this meant.

Began the process of healing, accepting what's not, started dealing, stopped living in the past that dropped me on my head, damn near killed me, almost left me for dead.

Pain is released when moving on, too long I held on when love was gone.

HOLINESS PROTECTS

Lord take away my blindness, help me discern the difference between manipulation and kindness.

Been misled and beguiled by a smiling face, while searching desperately for the sanctuary, that holy place.

The façade was shortened because you opened my eyes.

What appeared to be a house of worship was a den for profit, to my surprise.

It appeared to be genuine at first look, thank God I remembered when Isaiah said, "Read the book."

Some churches are more corporation than spreading the gospel of Yeshua, seeking vulnerable souls for personal gain, they need us.

Building up religion like it's completely big business, attempting to reel folks in like children at Christmas.

I'd think to myself how long had it been going on, until I received a message that was inappropriate, so wrong.

Disappointment and anger filled the essence of my soul, astonished at what I learned as I watched it revealed and unfold.

The enemy is clever, he confounds by our weakness, delivering fake emotions with rhetoric and vain speeches.

The holy spirit gives us comfort, discernment while he teaches.

Revealing unholy men seeking to drain our pockets like leaches.

According to my faith God's strength present while observing, I put my trust in God while continuing and serving.

The truth exclaims in his word, Yeshua is the truth, the way and the life, I'm steadfast, not moved by vain glory or provoked to senseless strife.

Praising the Lord God, no matter what the circumstances, been made whole by his blood, the God of second chances.

Vengeance is mine says the Lord, I will repay, those wolves in sheep clothing will be held accountable on judgment day.

Until that day I'll continue praying and fasting.

Nothing can separate God's love from us, it's everlasting.

My spirit sealed until the day of redemption, reconciled by just asking.

I'm in the world not of it, I'm peculiar as such, with spiritual maturing I don't get angry as much.

Praying for my enemies, loving them in spite of their way.

The holy spirit is a keeper and gives me what to say.

The battles are not mine, the enemy attempts to deceive, I stay focused on his word and continue to believe.

I may become disappointed at times emotional by the effects, yet always receiving goodness while the holiness protects.

I SAW YOU IN A DREAM

Wanting you so badly, to fall in love, madly, a whisper in my sleep.

I continued in my slumber, soundly I wonder, what passion of having you so deep.

Cradling my pillow, like child holds a teddy bear, in my mind, you were present, already there.

Imaginations running wild I can feel, even though I'm still sleeping, it's real.

I prayed for you, God inclined his ear, from a dream, one day you will appear.

Thoughts of your scent already saturating my senses, picturing you holding me tightly, sweet kisses, picket fences.

I see you standing there, my hearts pounding, butterflies in my stomach, it's hard to bare.

Aroused yet hypnotic, I'll lay here forever, waiting until I've got it.

Your stature tall, dark, mysteriously handsome and strong, reaching for you, forever it seems so long.

Cascading muscles from your arms to your feet, confident, no sign of conceit.

Warm inviting eyes, calling me by my name.

One touch from you I'll never be the same.

More rapidly my heart beating through my chest, staring at you, I'll need more rest.

Anticipation, complicating, my patience is starting to loose.

If I don't hold this moment hostage, the image of you could move.

Finally, what I've prayed for is about to evolve, no more lonely nights, happily involved.

Yet the hours are ticking away, soon I must awaken, fearing profoundly, my dream man will be taken.

As the sunlight invades my windows shade, I press harder, hoping my getting up will be delayed.

Purposely I move closer to you, my hand reaching for yours, wanting you with opening hearts, unlocking heavenly doors.

To have you in my life increasingly, I envision blissful days, loving you eternally, decently, impressed by all of your ways.

Morning is upon me, my dream slowly fading, at least I've had a taste of what I have been waiting.

Optionally I'll daydream seeing you in my mind, reality just around the corner, suspended in time.

I'm believing one day I'll meet you, like a dessert, I'll treat you, as well as complete you.

My prayers must come to pass, or I rather stay asleep in my bed so this dream will last.

A treasure to be found, made exclusively as I ask, God sending me my dream man not hard for him at all, a simple task.

As I need air to breathe, suddenly you can come, with me forever, and never leave.

Not knowing God's plan, yet preparing for what I shall receive.

Like the stars dance across a moonlit beam, soon you'll be here, I saw you in a dream.

INJURED SOUL

A broken heart and mental illness resembling, the likeness of a broken frame.

Diagnosed differently, yet without proper treatment, the issues remain.

Repeating the same behavior is called insanity if you expect a change, internal damage turns bitter when love does not exchange.

Our minds respond repetitiously, consistently without redirection, emotions enraged in need of counseling, the mirrored reflection.

Trust issues appear, for lack of true love and affection.

Desperation subjecting to reoccurring circumstances, familiarity a safety net.

Compromising reality, fearing what hasn't happened yet.

Changing the thought pattern, a difficult process, oh what a fight.

Struggling, emotionally driven far and beyond, the mind going from left turning right.

Fear will paralyze, reframing from thinking outside the box.

Courage will enlighten, encouraging a new, change unlocks.

In time a broken heart has a chance to mend.

Assessing competency or lack of in the mind without treatment can be the end.

Lost forever in a fragmented state, unable to comprehend reality from fantasy, no ability to relate.

Being the most needed organ, without the heart you're not able to live.

The absence of comprehendible thinking, the brain more sensitive.

Both critically needed for the body, they must be aligned, strategically with professional help, the saving just in time.

There are those lurking, seeking victims, vulnerable in search of affection, allowing their bodies to be used, for fear of rejection.

Not knowing, incapable of resisting, accepting unwarranted imperfection.

Mentally impaired isn't a moral characteristic, afflicted.

At times self-medicated, uncontrollably addicted.

Searching for satisfaction, never to be revealed impersonated, duplicated, engaging yet unfulfilled.

Dedicated to obtain a feeling impossible to describe, forced beyond control, delusional with a hostage trapped inside.

Perplexed, blaming everything and everyone envisioned by what's buried alive.

Detached through many crises, somehow able to survive.

Rational reasoning seems to be the missing link.

Success is relevant when mind, body, and soul working together, in sync.

Prayer changes many things regrets untold, healing is necessary to cure an injured soul.

IT'S OKAY TO SAY I'M NOT OKAY

Woke up with what felt like the weight of the world on my shoulder.

Could be because I'm menopausal, current situations and I'm getting older.

Emotions all over the place, although I try to hide, it still shows on my face.

Laying in my bed desperate for a peaceful place.

Seemingly I can't find it today, holding on by a thread reaching in an empty space.

Where is my joy, like many of my hidden issues packed away in an old suitcase?

Realizing that my feelings may be temporary, yet familiar so scary, unlocking a door makes my heart weary.

Honestly, plain to see at this moment I must say, for now, I'm not okay.

Memories of mistakes I've made, hearts that I've broken games that I played.

Haunting me taunting me, feeling dismayed, no sunshine only shade.

I try talking myself out of this funk, afraid of being afraid or looking like a punk.

The techniques I've used to deter my pain failed, debunked.

Finally admitting to myself without a doubt, I'm accepting I'm not always gonna be okay, then I begin to let it out.

Refraining from disclaiming, constantly renaming, no reason to continue blaming.

I must vent what I'm feeling, remorse from shaming, I'm not okay and so I'm saying.

Releasing myself from being the hostage, no way out unless I stop this.

Pending situations come and go as my life continues spinning, holding on to invisible ropes in hope that while in crisis I'm winning.

Faking what I feel doesn't make it go away, the baggage becomes heavier trying to keep it inside every day.

Realizing my truth peculiar as it may, facing me head-on, seeing a glimpse of the sun, the warmth in its ray, it's okay to say I'm not okay.

LEARNED BEHAVIOR

So use to doing things one way, unaware of circumstances influential each day.

Taught by the people you're surrounded by, no if's and's or but's about it, no lie.

Character traits transferred to vulnerable vessels, causing generational curses to exceed to higher levels.

Continuing on like a wrecking ball, setting up hidden agendas that makes us fall.

A closed mind acting out, systematically we're flawed, disemboweled, a learned behavior inherently taught and allowed.

Behaving in a manner thought to be regarded as acceptable, in reality missing the mark by a margin that's incredible.

Unfairly the writings on the wall were not legible.

Fear being the most common denominator, underestimated confusion comes without a translator.

When exposed to greater starting with an open mind, affecting the thought process, changing in time.

Recognizing red flags that previously went unnoticed, increasing positive results displaying a newness reshaping to mold us.

Engaging freely away from problematic episodes, intrigued by the lightening of our heavy loads.

Wisdom comes to those who are receptive, perpetuating repetitive inappropriate decisions now being selective.

Interpretations without knowledge damages the perspective.

Therefore, rendering damage to a soul, uncovered evidence, truth being told as it unfolds, from our beginnings eating out of African handmade bowls.

A tribe lost in search of a home, designations uncertain as they roam the unknown.

Incapable unable to dismiss their traditions, handed down similar unsavory conditions.

Unwilling as unyielding responding in irrevocable seditions.

There is a need beyond human ability transparent, a savior, supernatural means to get rid of unprofitable sometimes distasteful flavor.

Energy enhancing hypnotically entrancing, providing a waiver.

Escaping an attraction of an intentionally abstract distraction, accepting accountability for my learned behavior.

LIVING BENEFITS

Let me explain how you can win at this, preparation plus planning is legitimate.

A licensed agent will present products that fit, starting with an informative zoom call, 45-minutes, that's it.

The application process revealing your insurable interest.

Depending on your age including health issues that may exist.

The field underwriting agent using the application as a list.

Gathering necessary factors as the investigation permits.

The policy created only to indemnify, making you whole again you can rely.

A term policy for a period beneficial only if you die.

Be sure to be honest on your application, or the insurer will deny.

Leaving your loved ones a legacy the reason to apply.

Provisions casting down disparities less stress as you cry.

Living benefits accelerating the face amount is not a lie.

A valuable security that you can buy.

Premium payments decided the owner of the policy must comply.

Additional attractions are riders adding value, some free, others are paid by the owner at an additional fee.

Illustrations will be shown for the policy owner to see, also having cash accumulation sounds profitable to me.

Planning for the future brings peace to your mind, occasions can happen in an instant, at any time.

Yet living benefits guarantee my finances won't be in a bind.

There's no price you can place on your life, but we all should be covered, children, husband and wife.

Why be bogged down with financial woes that cut like a knife?

Being able to focus on recovering from an illness alone will suffice, being able to pay for my children's education without issues would be nice.

Deferred taxes yet another awesome feature, wealthy people have found ways to delay that creature.

Now, these opportunities are made available with no regrets, make the decision, and purchase a universal policy with living benefits.

MENOPAUSE

Agitated, irritated, I find myself crying without a true cause, I get hot as hell for no reason, Welcome to Menopause.

We are seasoned women entering into a new dimension with fixed incomes, awaking very early in the morning living on pensions.

We sometimes work part-time jobs with prices on essentials going up daily.

No overtime for me, I have to be wise of my spending with one check that they pay me.

This was supposed to be the time I relax in life, traveling and seeing wondrous sights, most of the time I can't sleep, tossing and turning through the night.

Health issues appear from out of nowhere, taking pills, and less energy.

I wonder to myself what in the world has happen to me.

My vision must be failing, I need reading glasses for small print.

Getting older, where did the young me go, wondering where my time went.

Don't run like I use to, calling young folks sweety, woke up two years ago with a medical emergency, diagnosed with diabetes.

I changed my diet, started exercising, sometimes hard to accept, the mind and body goes through many configurations the older you get.

You begin to see things much differently, you realize you have matured.

Thanking Yeshua each day with him I'm reassured.

Enjoying life with a new attitude, watching sunsets and simple pleasures.

What I use to take for granted, I definitely now treasure.

Moving forward in life, getting older is a blessing.

Yet it takes a little longer to prepare especially dressing.

Metaphorically and historically the fact will remain, if your blessed to get older, like seasons, everything will eventually change.

Yet grateful and at peace with getting older, I stop to take a pause, thank God I'm still alive, Welcome to Menopause.

MENTAL ILLNESS

The voices in my head have constantly kept me misled, its hard at times to sleep or get out the bed.

People are afraid of me, I sometimes have tendencies, my behavior unreasonable, judging me as crazy.

If I knew how to control this moment unexplained actions, the outburst, and distractions; my peace would be maximized with joy and utter satisfaction, just not able get it right in my head no matter how I try, suicide seems like an option, it may better if I die.

Feeling like an outcast, wondering how long this will last, the mood swings come and go extremely fast.

Calculating and continuously expressing my rage, nothing holding me back.

Paranoid, from the stares I get, now planning my attack.

You should stay out of my way when going through a crisis, it doesn't matter how kind you are, you could be the nicest.

In my mind, you're an enemy that can end up dead and lifeless.

Mental illness is not a moral deficiency, it's a health issue inside of me, that causes inappropriate behavior constantly.

Medication only eases the symptoms with no real escape, masking these unrealistic thoughts and actions I take.

All so troubling my condition is not rare, if you go to any major city, you see us wandering everywhere.

The government can fund wars and pay high salaries to politicians.

Why can't they help people like myself with this degenerative condition?

Until they find a cure guess I have to wait, hope they get a cure soon before it's too late.

You can't get angry with a person who has a medical condition such as cancer, we're not bad people, just left out, hoping for the answer.

THE MINDSET

Limitless boundaries to my thoughts I'm kept, searching through the mind's eye to see how far I'll get.

There's nothing in my way and nothing blocking my view, only visions of intentions on what I'd like to do.

Stopping isn't an option there's no program involved, I'll keep moving forward until all problems are solved.

The silence is so loud yet the ringing is so distracting.

My focus now changing to what appears to be attracting.

Looking at the sky and wondering why it's blue, I'm asking God why he made one and not two.

Perspective to my perception I'm always intrigued by the game.

I've lost count of how many times my position remained the same; captivated with curiosity the sun rays are so hot, I wonder how I get stuck over and over a lot.

My situation can't remain the same if in the end there is a lesson.

My dreams become reality when my mouth starts confessing.

I see myself in it without false hopes, even if I'm being beaten and up against the ropes.

Nothing is worthwhile if there is no struggle.

I endure the fight and can't knock the hustle.

I speak life even if I feel like I'm drowning, it's manifestation.

I'll keep swimming towards the shore a safe destination.

The spirit has muscle and gets stronger each time I cry.

I have no time for turning back or asking why.

My new life was created by a thought and a debt was paid.

The plan of greatness now being displayed.

My mind is like an airplane elevating, I won't stop.

My plan is to stay focused so the bottom doesn't drop.

Flexing with configurations that contort, relentless to make the effort a good report.

My mind made up and I'll win the bet, I'm believing the dream that begins with a determined mindset.

MY EX IS AN EXAMPLE OF WHAT I DON'T WANT ANYMORE

Guarding my peace is essential.

Keeping it in place gives grace to my mental.

Accepting applications for love, support a touch that caresses so gentle.

No longer will my tears fall like a flood to the floor,

Condoning a behavior I experienced before.

Again and again.

Begging someone to stay, instead of letting them walk out the door.

Clearly, our season together is over, and love don't live here anymore.

I'm better off on my own, not by myself with God's presence, I'm never alone.

Finding value in my tone, a vibe that satisfies and makes you moan.

Tired of playing kid games, a toxic-free zone, I want a partner, I'm grown.

And by the way I blocked my phone, even when I'm there, I ain't at home.

I saw the red flags yet I continued on, for fear of being without, the unknown.

So now I know, the hurt was ample, a loosing score.

My ex is an example of what I don't want anymore.

ON THE OTHER SIDE OF HARD IS SUCCESS

Anything and everything worthwhile is subject to a test.

Facing many obstacles on this road distracting, added stress.

Yet continuing on will one day find the hidden treasure chest.

Easy is not a possibility filled with sleepless nights, awaiting the manifest.

Although moving forward staying focused, continuing to confess.

Victory is mine, it's happening in God's time, won't settle for less.

Climbing mountains, reaching with strength and fitness, a no is a step closer to a yes.

Refusing to be defeated, as long as I rise in the morning, I'm blessed.

My past gave me courage with endurance, like a lion roaring, doing what's best.

Experience taught me lessons, in faith I know without having to guess.

What I envision, I look towards the goal ignoring the mess.

Situations requiring all of your muscle, beyond the limit, relentlessness.

Outlook may be vague, keeping your hustle, definitely possessing greatness.

Not moved by a difficult struggle, just keep trusting in who has kept me blessed.

Be steadfast unwavering, looking forward to unbridled complete happiness.

On the other side of hard is success.

OUTSIDE THE BOX

I'm more than a color, birthed by a teenage mother, limited to the opinions of another.

An original image beyond the stigma represented from that cover.

My skin has melanin exquisitely portioned like no other.

Jealous of how I look by your demonized perspective was chosen traditionally as selective.

Systematically classified as inferior, dutifully persistent proving to be more superior, judged only by the exterior.

It's been proven displayed directly in your face, even the thought of my kind exists forever, nothing can replace.

Being ridiculed because of wearing my hair in locks, wore them as many who's culture is outside the box.

Unstoppable raging in self-motivation not constrained by the hands on a clock.

Escaping the traps set before me, obstacles made to persuade me to stop.

A plan began surging forcefully in its intention to block, my memory takes me to the place reminding me I rock.

Running hard in a race that wasn't intended to be fair, I've already won just for being there.

How you see me isn't my business, self-induced division has you in despair.

Accepting myself as beautifully, wonderfully made to which nothing can compare.

I step out on faith to the plan that used to be forbidden, but by the grace of God, no longer am I hidden, nor am I angry, you are forgiven.

Opportunities may be difficult, larger than an ox, my application is succeeding from living outside the box.

PTSD

Loud noises are startling, the feeling of eminent death, mad for no apparent reason, constantly upset.

Suppressing my anger, paranoid in crowded rooms.

Unreasonable thoughts of gloom and doom.

Mood swings are normal, everyday feeling different wasn't unusual to me.

Finding out why this is happening, a disappointed moment, diagnosed with PTSD.

My thoughts traveled like winding roads, wicked, considered suicide.

Eluding reality, parts of me quite damaged on the inside.

Consistently ruled by fear, confusion, abused an extremely horrified.

Frustrated, elated, in denial regarding this unexpected diagnoses, completely unable to be successful with romantic closeness.

Believing I'd fail no matter how good things were going, sabotage seemingly the remedy.

Couldn't believe in love without pain, just didn't seem real to me.

Finally, it was revealed to me, an unconditional love that's given freely.

Yeshua the risen savior, full of mercy, grace unmerited sufficiently.

Freedom unparalleled, a light at the end of a darkened tunnel, redeemed.

My emotional outburst made sense, learning a sense of peace, released it seemed.

Though I fight this battle with tenacity, my restless nights haven't gone away.

At least I don't feel as lost, no hope, or left astray.

I find myself taking medication to ease these unbearable symptoms, not nearly as strained.

Even when I feel that someone is out to get me, that feeling is explained.

No longer embarrassed, nor ignoring a pain that's real.

Found out many others suffer just as I do knowing exactly how I feel.

Gratifying yet empathic this chronic rollercoaster has kept my guard up, protecting.

Allowing more people into my heart without being afraid, subjecting.

Stopped pushing away those who understand wanting to be a friend.

Forcing myself to have faith in God, his will for me, my expected end.

Memories still haunt me and I fight with new coping skills, breathing deeply, relaxing my mind without losing total control, God's love heals so sweetly.

Desperation, defeat, self-hatred a terrible concept when desiring better, listening to calming music, even talking myself off the ledge, sometimes writing a letter.

Therapy teaches a healthier way to deal with this issue, some days I go through a whole box of tissue.

Today I feel victorious not just crazy as I've been called, relying more on Yeshua, not so much appalled.

Hoping medical science will someday find a cure, accepting my condition is a medical diagnosis, my heart is surely pure.

PUNISHMENT MINUS LOVE IS TYRANNY

Those crushing blows didn't teach respect, replaced anger a disconnect.

Tried ignoring broken pieces as I reflect, explaining bruises left on my neck.

Self-medicated to disguise the wreck, the idea of love untrustworthy, I reject.

Affection shown indirectly occasionally correct, insufficient amounts do neglect.

Mentally inferior ruining an object, confusing the spirit now battered, in debt.

Attempting to engage though really upset, not understanding how angry you get.

Fear is a mechanism used to deflect, correction in love builds character without regret.

Rebuilding the brokenness of an original project, good luck to you in winning that bet.

Tremendous effort, needing gross less the net, hoping help arrives enabling to reset.

Infusing harsh repercussions, you'll never forget, turning the pages burning like a cigarette.

Yet coming into the world planned not as a threat, disturbing
methods mishandling epithet.

Disposition cold from resentment, added fear in me,
punishment minus love is tyranny.

RELENTLESSLY BROWN

Are you mad because I'm made with purpose, beautiful and brown, not just on the surface?

Does my confidence and intelligence confuse you and make you feel worthless?

Do my curves threaten you, filling your mind with stress?

Are you mad because of the way I fill out this dress?

You try and copy me but are so unwilling to confess.

It drives you crazy, even you know I'm the best.

Can't take your eyes off me, my presence is so lovely.

The hatred in your heart and mind is what makes you ugly.

I know it's hard for you to comprehend, fronting like you wanna be my friend.

The demise you planned for me is actually your expected end.

I know you're jealous, I can see you.

I'm watching from a distance in my rearview.

What's most difficult for you to accept in reality, God's plan for my greatness.

Try praying more for yourself and hating on me less.

What's been given to me is gifted and strength beyond your comprehension.

If you would learn my history and listen, quit lying and pay attention.

Just release the hatred you've always had, passed down from your mom and dad.

Always attempting to steal what we've already had.

It's not a competition, you're just mad.

I've already won, no matter how devious the plot, it was planned from the beginning, something you can't stop.

Learn the truth about me, quit trying to devalue what's gold.

Believe the real history that you haven't been told.

It's time for all of my people to be unafraid and heal, the real reason Colin Kaepernick chose to kneel.

So give it up with your secret agendas and plans to kill, no matter how much blood you maliciously try to spill.

You thirst for what I have, even my ideals.

You could never conceive what we've been through or what we feel.

Confidence and love is how I stand with boldness, rhetoric, lies and jealousy reflects your overbearing coldness.

No more explanations you can't knock me down.

By now you should know, I'm relentlessly brown.

SCHEDULED FOR A SEASON

Manifested unexpectedly by design according to the vision.

Not determined by the hands on a clock, a spiritual decision.

Beyond assumptions derived in the minds, overshadowing a mere desire.

Powers above evolving from beyond thoughts, created much higher.

What we perceive is in our reach, yet with patience, awaiting while we seek.

Clinging to our faith, being humbled, learning as we teach.

Our plans may not come to pass at a desired day.

Delaying may reverse the curse that will come to destroy, dismantle, or dismay.

The process is rooted not changing, designated on time by claiming.

Blessings are scheduled within a specific season with naming.

Being prepared for what you ask, a defining level of gratitude.

Building from inside your spirit, eliminating anxiety, baring good fruit by a positive attitude.

Discomfort must be confronted adjusting positioning, blessings guaranteed.

Credible evidence will be revealed, not superficially, only supplying what we need.

Tables do turn, our thoughts provoking, giving ability to discern.

Believing that which is hoped for, grace is given not earned.

Planting seeds, speaking life over all that's instore for me.

God's promises essential, definite, occurring on that predestinated day I'll see.

Exceeding in reality, giving me more than I planned for.

Windows overflowing, never shutting, expectations, engaged through an open door.

Success is not measured by how quickly we set a predetermined date.

Young or old, blessings continue to flow, receiving in time not too late.

Influenced, confessing unquestionable reasoning, embodied an enlightened for greater is inside of me.

Exposing what's already done, a heartfelt expectancy.

A perfect fit, no limits, arriving in its certainty, shattering all doubt.

Making room endowed with empowerment, lacking nothing nor going without.

My past an image uncompromised, encountered for a reason, no time has been wasted, all scheduled for a season.

SINGLE MAMA

Girl I know this is not what you planned, having a baby alone, without his dad.

You actually wish you could take back the day you met his sorry butt, I'm sure you wish you had.

All those broken promises, misleading you, talking all that sweet talk.

The baby been here 3 months this bum hasn't called, he decided to take a walk.

Right out of your life, doesn't consider how bad you must feel.

Best believe the thought of running up with a baseball bat, that feeling so real.

Every time you look at your new baby, you see the remarkable resemblance.

Can't understand how you can walk out on your own flesh and blood, the lies he told, remembrance.

Trying your best to put on the façade that it's all good, you got this.

Though the real truth being, your feeling abandoned, betrayed, now having trust issues, situation ruthless.

You begin to blame yourself, saying I must of did something wrong, I fell in love to quick.

Why on earth is this happening to me, I'm so embarrassed, I really thought we clicked.

The problem isn't always your fault, these situations aren't rare, so many baby mama's.

You just thought you had the perfect guy and wasn't prepared for this kind of drama.

Resentment sets in its gonna be so hard to let your guard down, you say never again.

In the beginning of any real relationship, it's best to make that man a friend.

Examining how he lives his life, is he good to his own mama, ask about other females he's dated, how many of them are suffering the same trauma.

Dudes like this usually show red flags if you pay very close attention, how they refer to previous women from their past, just sit back and listen.

You have to be two steps ahead and be sure to always love yourself first, no one wants this generational havoc following them, it's a curse.

Teaching your children self-love day and night reiterate, God is always first in your life, the only one that will validate.

Stop beating yourself up, look forward to a greater future, focus on that child.

Leave these men alone, not forever, yet at least a while.

Give yourself a chance, heal, leaving all regrets behind.

Your baby was born on purpose, take the necessary time to reconcile with self, never believe you're worthless.

There may come a time when this man may want to reenter your life, pump your breaks.

Trust is earned not freely given, let's see the effort he's willing to make, you don't wanna end up repeating the same mistakes.

Thank God for the lesson you learned, a baby is a blessing.

Remember to make sure that man can't live without you, no more second-guessing.

Children need both parents, it takes two to conceive it's required, a moment of passion will turn into something else, from what you sexually desired.

STRONG BLACK WOMAN

Goes to work even if she's sick, will catch a bus, take a cab or walk with a big stick, Strong Black Woman, her mind is beautiful, intelligent, and bold.

Her skin doesn't crack, not even when she is old.

If you listen and watch, her story is captured and told.

Her conversation strong, black, and bold.

Even over 60 her strength and body is cold.

Strong Black Woman, she leads and teaches her children, with life lessons that will fill them, provides nurturing, loving and commits, no time for foolishness, no time for it.

Strong Black Woman, hides her pain, frustration, sacrifices with strain.

Constantly moving forward, hardly ever complains.

She's got things to do, no time for games.

Strong Black Woman, strapped up with a full figure, thin in the middle, bottom much bigger, if you mess with her family or money, she might have her finger on that trigger.

Strong Black Woman, don't piss her off or make her mad, the cussin may come quick, she'll make you wish you had, a second chance to take back what you said.

Her main concern is keeping her family fed.

Strong Black Woman, toe to toe you're not able to match her tongue, she's been gangsta since she was young, she's that girl that will leave you standing there looking dumb.

Strong Black Woman, you've been riddled with pain, raped but never tamed, put "Ms." In front when you call her name.

SWEET STREET SISTAH...

Growing up on the mean streets, ghetto living in Chicago, flowing with rhythmic beats the way her swag goes.

Creating energy that sounds good to the ears, the magic of her music methodically engagingly sincere.

Rocking the mic enlightened by her vision, each verse a work of art like a surgeon, making an incision hot like fire the intensity cultivating a raging desire, wanting more like good weed taking you higher.

It's no coincidence baby been bad since birth, she'll have ya bobbin ya head until she leaves this earth.

True indeed, this is a man's world, you ain't seen nothing until you rock with oh girl.

Sweet Street Sistah holding it down like only you can do it, can't explain the struggle, looking like you haven't been through it.

Young black and gifted, feeling her groove, glad you didn't miss it, her sound is the move.

Sexy slim easy on the eyes, loving what you're doin is no surprise, got the people in her audience hypnotized.

Talented in her lane, forever she will remain, masterpieces that will change the game.

A genius at her craft determined to make her mark, never gave it up, that part.

So sit back and listen, see the precision in her decision to always be great.

Left those streets alone before it was too late.

Hip hop has made many millionaires, pay attention to this lyricist giant as she prepares.

Reaching incredible heights only by superstars, keeping it fresh to death while buying new cars.

So, morale of this story has a twista, put ya hands together for a Sweet Street Sistah.

TABLES TURN AS BRIDGES BURN

Closed doors open as lessons confirm, unsavory intentions send destructive energy in return.

Unresolved issues attacking compassionate souls without concern.

Vicious cycles inevitable until they learn.

Temporarily seducing each hostage displaying an evil smile, contradictive personalities confuse as they beguile, a reputation of deception creative in its style.

Devouring fragile unsuspecting people held captive for a while.

A seed produces a harvest revealing your turn, miraculously tables turn as bridges burn.

Life will write the checks you deserve as you earn.

Spiritual beings recognize your demise with their discern.

Unwilling to compromise their lives this session adjourn.

Being proactive, released like hair relaxing from a perm.

Enough time has been spent, you in my head not paying rent.

Dismissing demonic forces were crucially evident, replaced by peace a chosen resident.

Some call it karma let me reaffirm, be mindful tables turn as bridges burn.

ITS MY BUSINESS

What I do and like has nothing to do with you, obviously there's too much time on your hands boo.

Why do you care, stop counting my pockets no way for you to compare?

Be concerned with your bank accounts, oops nothing is there.

Maybe if you paid more attention, quit trying to be a witness, I do what I want with intention, it's my business.

Talking about people behind their back, your truth is vague not based on a fact.

You better check yourself and stay the hell back.

Pretending you have it all together when in reality you're crap wack as ever.

Mad because you're not like me a buried treasure.

Looking for attention at the expense of others, always trying to mention irrelevant stories regarding another.

Talk about your life I know it's a shortlist, the part you fail to realize, I'm not interested, it's your business.

No concerns for things I'm not involved in, you're tired a waste of time with issues, try to solve them.

Get out of my face with that B.S. your world revolves in.

My goals are tangible you can't get with this, so out touch, facts, it's my business.

Go get you some business while you stay out of mine, you are too old for this crap stop wasting my time.

At some point you will find, all the time you've spent made you blind.

Your efforts to discredit was so unkind.

Still the stories you told never affected what's mine.

My blessings will come no matter what you speak, I'm covered by the master from my head to my feet.

Try moving in silence trapped in your inner violence, enable to be discrete.

Captivated in amazement your incapable, lil creep.

Your heart burns with jealousy knowing I'm so sweet.

So, sit yo ass down as you listen to this, don't worry about me darlin, that's my business.

Not carrying on like a fool, I'm building wealth my faith is a tool.

Making plans, that you'll never understand, keep watching as I rule.

Feeling sorry for you, it's hard for you to take this.

You're just a carbon copy, I know you hate this.

You can't stop my greatness, a simple reason why, it's my fate to be in this, it's my business.

THE MASTER'S HANDS

Created in his image intentions designated in his purpose
displayed by you from the start, purposely revealing your
uncompromising integrity envisioned a sweet genuine heart.

Not to mention the brilliance of your absolute being,
originated and orchestrated as a work of art.

Demonstrating in its perfected election, achieving sublimed
stamina authenticating your selection.

Reminding you of the position ordained in your creation,
calculated through the desire in his manifestation.

Let your steps move with the regal elegance seen through the
eyes, represented in the apparent necessity of your presence
implied no disguise.

Inherently describing a mystic unfabricated blueprint
realizing greatness resembling no lies.

Esteemed with overwhelming depictions glorified abilities
supernaturally defies, reasoning unblemished from
questionable afflictions perpetuated for your demise.

Rejecting those implications from intimidated frustrations,
motivated by strengths casting down reoccurring occasions.

Ratified while gratified defined as wonderful by his
demonstrations.

Understanding as to commanding to conscious acceptance flowing through revelations.

Your fragrant essence, intertwined curves projected illustrations, illuding to sensuous sensations.

Vibrant energy infectious yet charismatic so inviting in its interpretations.

Attractively stimulating, empowering anticipating, inspiring for those willingly waiting.

Captivated though intrigued, contemplating before received, enticed by what's perceived.

Your portion given by whom they believed.

Bringing value exclusively established by his plans, thank God for a woman's existence, erected from the master's hands.

THE NARCISSIST

At times you'll come in contact with people, takers who are jealous of your gifts.

The reason behind this defective character, the reality is your dealing with a narcissist.

Completely self-absorbed, only concerned with their own situation, every conversation reverts to them again and again.

Always disagreeing when information exceeds their limited understanding.

Never satisfied, ungrateful, always complaining, so demanding.

It's always someone else's fault when things are going wrong.

Like listening to a broken record stuck on the same song.

When tragedy strikes they will need all of your attention, yet when you have important issues, they won't make time to listen.

Extremely selfish, appearing to be concerned, before you can blink they've already turned.

Nowhere to be found unless it's convenient, at best.

Nothing matters to them as you realize, easy to assess.

Relentless when talking, will tell the best stories, loves debating.

They will constantly overtalk you, cut you off, so frustrating.

Whatever the topic they must make an attempt to control it and compete.

In their small minds they believe it's a competition, they can't handle defeat.

Covetous, envious when they are not a part of your prosperity.

Unwilling to celebrate you 100% because of their own insecurity.

Moody and often unfriendly at times depending on the weather.

If a situation doesn't make them look good, their attitude is, "Whatever!"

When confronting them with these mentally unstable flaws, they will turn it around, blame you like you've broken laws.

Having no problems revealing all your personal secrets, so disloyal.

At the mention of any of their negative past behavior, you will be watching their blood boil.

Constantly living in a deep-rooted denial.

As far as they're concerned, they deleted that file.

Very difficult to navigate with a narcissist on your team.

These are damaged people with a lack of genuine self-esteem.

Exasperating actors will display much drama, having no regret.

The more you do for a narcissist the more they will neglect, only remaining in your circle to defocus and deflect.

One of their consistent traits is playing the victims, self-inflicted wounds, hidden agendas, no real symptoms.

Recognize the character of these people with this ability, mostly immature, unyielding, taking no thought for assuming responsibility.

Pay close attention, and remember this, you're dealing with a control freak, a narcissist.

TOXIC

Based on my relationships, all so unhealthy unable to stop it, too afraid to be just me, couldn't drop it.

Over and over repeated bad behavior seeing others, I mocked it.

Not many positive examples to follow looking through a broken frame I cropped it.

Emulating the visions through clouded eyes I became toxic.

Years of resentment filled with hatred, self-inflicting wounds, tears cascaded.

Self-medicating escaping reality kept me falsely elated.

Still, my life raging out of control, drugs masked the pain but I sold my soul.

Didn't realize the size as I dug the hole.

Abrasions unveiled a shattered mold.

Most times I felt lost left out in the cold.

It started as a child about 5 years old.

Learning I was adopted caused feelings of abandonment, screaming for attention bad or good I was adamant.

Accepting crumbs from a pocket, nothing seemed to block it.

This damaged little girl now toxic.

Trying to be what people expected, no self-esteem could not be detected.

Everything I touched became infected.

Not used to unconditional love, so I rejected.

Becoming my worst enemy with negative energy I deflected.

Transferring my anger shifting what I projected.

Saturated others with a never-ending storm purposely subjected.

As the episodes increased progressively yet chronic, I'd use humor disguised as a comic.

Truth is I graduated to being neurotic.

My thoughts of inadequacy intensified impaired logic, not loving me made my life chaotic, healing comes by confessing and discussing topics, overcoming trauma that can leave you toxic.

WHAT IF

I look into your eyes instead of the color of your skin, make a decision to love you not judge you and just be your friend.

What if, I ran with you, helped you leap over a hurdle.

Be patient, steadfast, hold you tight like grandma's girdle.

What if, I fed you, hugged you, gave you a warm loving gift, instead of hating you and beating you with my fist.

What if, we unite, fight together get tight, shine like a lighthouse at night.

Move forward instead of backward, help elevate each other no matters who's right.

What if, we plan a meal, break bread eat, communicate, instead.

You bring something, I bring something, everybody's fed.

Stop comparing, criticizing, quit being misled.

What if, I share with you like a brother, when you have a need, sow seeds like family, having the same mother.

Listen to you with compassion, redirect when I know to do better, when I see you standing there shivering, give you my sweater.

What if, I aid you in getting back on your feet, instead of looking down at you and leave you in the street.

Share my knowledge when I consider your need, not try to take everything for myself motivated by greed.

What if, I invite you to my home, I know you're homeless, treat you like family, giving you my best, stand by your side allow you to rest.

What if, I find you crying standing in the rain, let you use my umbrella while you explain the reason for your pain, encourage you after I listen, extend a hand until you regain.

Be patient, wait for you, identify, and don't complain.

What if, I hurt you with my actions, apologize, repent hoping to be forgiven.

You accept promises are kept, back to righteous living.

Prayer changes everything, people deserve second chances, when we use positive energy, greater tends to happen.

What if, we change our position on the past, reconcile in our disposition, agree to escape from hateful traditions, making empathetic reasoning through wisdom, changing our condition.

What if, we make a conscious effort to transform, having a renewing of our mind, treat all people equally, one race, mankind.

Love unconditionally with a sweet intention looking for nothing in return.

What if, we show true remorse for our unkind gestures, remembering what we've learned.

WOUNDS INTO WISDOM

Social media won't let some rest, no more intimate communications, we'd rather text.

Proclaiming a life unrealistic, superficial narrative is what we suggest.

Hiding behind broken spirits, normalizing pain from regrets.

Afraid to be honest fearing what's next, strength comes from within healing from wounds is the real flex.

Leaving past hurt behind moving towards a positive vision.

Being true to ourselves turns wounds into wisdom.

Rejecting paralyzing images unwilling to succumb.

Refusing to repeat similar behavior expecting a difference to come.

Scars remind you, faith with endurance defines you.

Refrain from negative mindsets that only came to rewind you.

Troubles don't last always, teaching us lessons revealing better days, at times we feel lost trapped in a maze.

Believe in yourself, God provides open doors guiding the ways.

Living life by a standard competing with myself, never others.

My mistakes made me who I am, pulling back the covers.

Having patience allowing time for making room.

Wisdom is present when healing covers the wound.

Expectations are met no reasons to assume, pouring salt on the laceration brings bitterness and gloom.

Humbly we ignite, preferring God to fight, the battle came by day and left last night.

No giving in, the struggle is real, no matter what happens, my perspective decides how I deal.

Choosing to be better revisiting those scarred hands, releasing the anger, implementing greater plans.

A smooth stone can cause major damage, getting out the way enlightens so I can manage.

Getting older leaving stages set for me to mature.

Listening intensely remembering I'm sure.

The flex in my talk abounds in my walk, I can go a million miles from what I've been taught.

It's not always easy nor is it fun, yet waiting for healing is the beginning of turning wounds into wisdom.

Made in the USA
Monee, IL
26 April 2022

95450904R00069